WORLD MYTHOLOGY

DIANA

Adele D. Richardson

Consultant:
Dr. Laurel Bowman
Department of Greek and Roman Studies
University of Victoria, British Columbia

Capstone
press

Mankato, Minnesota

Capstone Press
151 Good Counsel Drive, P.O. Box 669, Mankato, Minnesota 56002
http://www.capstone-press.com

Library of Congress Cataloging-in-Publication Data
Richardson, Adele, 1966–
    Diana / Adele D. Richardson.
    p. cm.—(World mythology)
    Summary: Relates the exploits of Diana and her importance in Roman mythology,
including her connection to such figures as Actaeon and Orion, and describes the role of
myths in the modern world.
    Includes bibliographical references and index.
    ISBN 0-7368-1609-7 (hardcover)
    1. Diana (Roman deity)—Juvenile literature. [1. Diana (Roman deity) 2. Mythology,
Roman.] I. Title. II. Series.
BL820.D5 R53 2003
292.2'114—dc21
                      2002008462

Editorial Credits

Blake A. Hoena, editor; Karen Risch, product planning editor; Juliette Peters, designer and
    illustrator; Alta Schaffer, photo researcher

Photo Credits

Art Resource/Réunion des Musées Nationaux, 4; SEF, 6; Giraudon, 8, 20 (left);
    Eric Lessing, 10; Scala, 14
Corbis/Gian Berto Vanni, cover; Stapleton Collection, 16; Arte & Immagini srl, 18
Digital Vision Ltd., 20 (right)

1 2 3 4 5 6 08 07 06 05 04 03

TABLE OF CONTENTS

4

Artwork often shows Diana with a deer or a hunting dog. She usually is carrying a bow and arrows. These animals and items represent hunting.

DIANA

In Roman myths, Diana was the goddess of the hunt and the Moon. She was the chief hunter among the gods. No god or person could hunt better than Diana could. In Greek myths, Diana is known as Artemis (AR-tuh-muhss).

Diana also was the goddess of forests, animals, and childbirth. She especially loved forests of oak and cypress trees. Ancient Romans believed Diana protected animals and children.

Diana was one of the Olympians. Ancient Greeks and Romans believed these 12 powerful gods ruled the world from Mount Olympus. This mountain is in central Greece. Ancient Greeks and Romans believed the gods controlled every part of their lives.

Ancient Greeks and Romans built many temples for their gods. This temple in Jerash, Jordan, honors Artemis (Greek for Diana). It was built around A.D. 200.

ABOUT MYTHOLOGY

The word myth comes from the Greek word *mythos*. It means word or story. Mythology is the retelling of stories.

Myths show how people understood the world. Ancient Greeks and Romans told myths to explain why things happened. Some myths explained why flowers bloomed in the spring or why the sun moved across the sky. Other myths told how the world and the gods were created.

Many of the characters in myths were gods. Ancient Greeks and Romans believed the gods controlled everything that happened in nature.

Ancient Greeks and Romans believed gods such as Diana were real. Romans built temples for Diana. They brought food and treasures to the temples to honor her. They prayed to her for help. People asked Diana for a successful hunt. Women asked her for a safe childbirth.

This ancient vase shows a scene from the myth of Niobe. Niobe had angered Diana (left) and Apollo (right). Niobe said that she was a better mother than Latona. She had 14 children. Latona only had two. In anger, the twin gods killed Niobe's children.

THE BIRTH OF DIANA

Diana's father was Jupiter (JOO-puh-tur). He was the ruler of the Olympians and the father of many gods.

Jupiter was married to Juno (JOO-noh). He was not a loyal husband. He fell in love with the Titaness Latona (luh-TOH-nah). Juno was angry when Latona became pregnant with Jupiter's twin children. She chased Latona all over the world. Juno would not let Latona give birth to her children on the earth.

Latona finally went to Delos (DEH-lohss). In myths, this rocky island floated above the sea. Latona gave birth to Diana on Delos. After her birth, Diana helped Latona give birth to her twin brother. Latona named her son Apollo (uh-PAH-loh). Apollo became the god of youth and music.

Diana and Apollo were both very beautiful. Myths say that Apollo was surrounded by golden light. Diana shone with silver light like the Moon.

Myths say that Diana spent much of her time hunting.
Jan Fyt's painting *Diana's Hunt* shows her with nymphs
and her hunting dogs after a hunt.

DIANA'S BIRTHDAY WISHES

Jupiter loved Diana very much. On her third birthday, he asked her to make some wishes. He said he would give her whatever she wanted. Diana told Jupiter that she wished for three things.

First, Diana asked to stay young. She never wanted to grow up into a woman or get married. Jupiter allowed her to stay young forever. Diana never married, and she never had any children.

Next, Diana wished for a silver bow and arrows. Jupiter had his son Vulcan (VUHL-kan) make her magic arrows. Animals died without feeling any pain when struck by these arrows.

Lastly, Diana asked for a pack of hunting dogs. Jupiter gave her 10 of the world's best hunting dogs. Diana spent her days and nights hunting with them.

GREEK and ROMAN *Mythical Figures*

Greek Name: **APOLLO**
Roman Name: **APOLLO**
Diana's brother and god of
youth and music

Greek Name: **ARTEMIS**
Roman Name: **DIANA**
Zeus' daughter and goddess of
the hunt and the Moon

Greek Name: **HEPHAESTUS**
Roman Name: **VULCAN**
Zeus' son and god of fire

Greek Name: **HERA**
Roman Name: **JUNO**
Zeus' wife and goddess of
marriage and childbirth

Greek Name: **HERACLES**
Roman Name: **HERCULES**
Greek hero famous for performing
his 12 labors

Greek Name: **LETO**
Roman Name: **LATONA**
Diana's mother

Greek Name: **ZEUS**
Roman Name: **JUPITER**
Diana's father and ruler of
the Olympians

THE TELLING OF MYTHS

Historians believe the Greeks told the first myths about Artemis (Greek for Diana) around 2000 B.C. At the time, people did not know how to read or write. Children often gathered around their parents or grandparents to hear stories about Artemis. When the children grew up, they told the same stories to their children.

Storytellers also told myths. These people wandered from village to village telling the myths to large crowds. Storytellers often changed the myths as they told them. They told the myths in different ways to make them more exciting. Today, there may be several versions of the same myth because of the storytellers' changes.

The Romans captured Greece around 100 B.C. The Romans liked the myths they heard in Greece. They adopted many Greek myths as their own. The Romans often connected their own gods to Greeks gods. The Greek goddess Artemis became known as the Roman goddess Diana. The Greek god Zeus was called Jupiter by the Romans.

In myths, gods often punished people who made them angry. Diana
turned Actaeon into a deer for watching her bathe. This painting
shows Actaeon as a deer being attacked by his hunting dogs.

DIANA AND ACTAEON

The story of Actaeon (ak-TEE-uhn) was a popular myth told by storytellers. Actaeon was a prince of Thebes, Greece.

Actaeon often hunted with his hunting dogs in the woods near his home. One night, he saw a strange group of trees. He had never seen this grove before and decided to explore it.

After entering the grove, Actaeon saw a moonlit lake. Diana and some nymphs were bathing in the water. Actaeon watched Diana. He was amazed by her beauty.

The nymphs saw Actaeon. They crowded around Diana to cover her up with clothes.

Diana was angry at Actaeon for watching her bathe. She threw a handful of water at him. Actaeon turned into a deer as soon as the water touched him.

Actaeon then became afraid and ran away. Actaeon's hunting dogs saw him running. They did not recognize him because he was a deer. The dogs chased Actaeon and killed him.

The constellation Orion the Hunter is easily found in the night sky. A row of three bright stars forms Orion's belt. Other bright stars represent his shoulders and legs.

DIANA AND ORION

Diana and Apollo spent a great deal of time together. The only other man Diana liked spending time with was the giant Orion (oh-RYE-uhn). He was her cousin and a skilled hunter. Diana and Orion spent many nights hunting together.

Apollo loved his twin sister very much. He was jealous of the time Diana spent with Orion. In anger, Apollo sent a scorpion to sting Orion. The scorpion stung the giant on the heel of his foot. Its poison killed Orion.

Diana was saddened by Orion's death. She went to Jupiter and asked him to place Orion's body in the night sky. She then could see him at night when she hunted.

Jupiter did as Diana asked. In the sky, Orion became known as the constellation Orion the Hunter. Beside Orion, Jupiter placed the scorpion that stung Orion. This constellation is called Scorpio.

King Eurystheus
(yoo-RISS-thee-uhss)
gave Hercules
12 labors. Hercules
performed these tasks
to be forgiven for
killing his wife and
children. He captured
the Cerynitian Stag
for his third labor.

HERCULES AND DIANA'S STAG

Hercules (HUR-kyoo-leez) was a great hero in myths. He was famous for performing his 12 labors. For one of these tasks, he had to catch the Cerynitian (sur-i-NEE-tee-uhn) Stag. This white deer had golden horns and was important to Diana.

The deer was very fast and strong. Hercules chased it for one year before it finally grew tired. He then caught it and tied its legs together.

Diana suddenly appeared before Hercules. She was angry at him for capturing her sacred deer. Hercules begged her not to harm him. He explained that he had to catch the Cerynitian Stag for one of his 12 labors. He also promised to set the deer free once his task was complete.

Diana trusted Hercules. He was known for helping people and doing good deeds. Diana forgave Hercules and let him leave with the deer. Hercules kept his promise and let the Cerynitian Stag go after completing his task.

People can see this statue of Diana (left) in the Louvre art museum in Paris, France. Diana was the goddess of the Moon (below). Myths say she often hunted at night by the light of the Moon.

MYTHOLOGY TODAY

People no longer believe in the power of Greek and Roman gods. But myths still have an influence today. The planets in our solar system are named after Roman gods. The largest planet is named Jupiter after the ruler of the Olympians. Places also share the names of mythical figures. Texas and West Virginia both have cities called Diana.

People use names from myths. Diana is a common name. It means "divine," or "godlike." Diane, Deanna, and Diandra are other names that come from the Roman goddess of hunting.

Myths also influence artists. For thousands of years, artists have created paintings and sculptures about mythical figures. These works of art can be seen in museums around the world.

Today, people tell myths for their enjoyment. Movies have been made about popular myths. Authors have retold myths in books. Myths are interesting and exciting stories.

Adriatic Sea

•Rome

ITALY

N
W • E
S

GREECE

Troy

Aegean Sea

Thebes

ITHACA

Athens

Ionian Sea

Sparta

DELOS

SCALE
Miles
0   100   200

0   100   200
Kilometers

KEY

•   City

Oracle of Delphi

Mount Olympus

Region of Attica

CRETE

Mediterranean Sea

WORDS TO KNOW

adopt (uh-DOPT)—to accept an idea or a way of doing things

ancient (AYN-shunt)—very old

constellation (kon-stuh-LAY-shuhn)—a group of stars that forms a shape

immortal (i-MOR-tuhl)—able to live forever

nymph (NIMF)—a female spirit or goddess found in a meadow, a forest, a mountain, or a stream

Olympian (oh-LIM-pee-uhn)—one of the 12 powerful gods who lived on Mount Olympus in Greece

sacred (SAY-krid)—very important to someone

stag (STAG)—an adult male deer

temple (TEM-puhl)—a building used for worship

Titan (TYE-ten)—one of the giants who ruled the world before the Olympians

READ MORE

McCaughrean, Geraldine. *Roman Myths.* New York: Margaret McElderry Books, 2001.

Richardson, Adele D. *Hercules.* World Mythology. Mankato, Minn.: Capstone Press, 2003.

USEFUL ADDRESSES

National Junior Classical League
Miami University
Oxford, OH 45056

Ontario Classical Association
2072 Madden Boulevard
Oakville, ON L6H 3L6
Canada

INTERNET SITES

Track down many sites about Diana.
Visit the FACT HOUND at *http://www.facthound.com*

IT IS EASY! IT IS FUN!

1) Go to *http://www.facthound.com*
2) Type in: 0736816097
3) Click on "FETCH IT" and FACT HOUND
will find several links hand-picked by our editors.

Relax and let our pal FACT HOUND do the research for you!

INDEX